GHOSTS OF THE SEVEN SEAS

Written by:
Stuart Kallen

Published by Abdo & Daughters, 6535 Cecilia Circle, Edina, Minnesota 55439.

Library bound edition distributed by Rockbottom Books, Pentagon Tower, P.O. Box 36036, Minneapolis, Minnesota 55435.

Library of Congress Number: 91-073060   ISBN: 1-56239-041-4

Cover Illustration by: Tim Blough
Interiors by: Tim Blough

Edited by: Rosemary Wallner

TABLE OF CONTENTS

WRAITHS OF THE WIND

The year is 1827. The place is the Dogger Bank, a shallow stretch of the North Sea between England and Denmark. It is night watch on the good ship *Maria.* A tired sailor keeps a weary eye out for storms and pirates. His telescope is close at hand to scan the horizon for any passing ships. A flare gun is loaded to signal any other ship of calamity. The snores of the sailor's shipmates drift above deck and the night is a starry dome. When the new moon rises, its horns are pointed upward so it appears as a bowl from which fresh water will spill—a sure sign that the weather will be fair.

As the evening winds blow fresh from the south, the ship's ropes hit lightly against the masts and the water whispers gently by the hull. The massive ship groans with every passing wave. At midnight, the lantern casts a yellow pool of light across the glistening decks, and the shadows shiver with the rocking sea.

Suddenly, something takes shape in the water and rises swiftly into the air. Dancing out of the waves, figures of pale men appear, their faces shining wet with water and their clothes hanging in tattered, dripping rags. The sailor's shipmates rush to the deck, but stand frozen in terror as the sunken-eyed wraiths stare at them.

Like flames rising into the night, the apparitions rise silently from the water. Their bony fingers grab the ship's gunwales, and they heave themselves onto the deck. Ignoring the sailors, the ghosts walk past them and take up positions on the ship. Their expressions are empty and blind. One ghost takes over the wheel, his hands moving over it like he is steering—but the wheel remains motionless. Two other phantoms unwind invisible nets and cast them to the sea. Working in unison, they haul the nets in, but there are no fish. After what seems like an endless amount of time, the ghosts fade into the air, leaving the shaking sailors staring at nothing.

The men who witnessed the phantom sailors tell their captain what they have seen. He shrugs and tells them to go back to sleep. The captain knows what the ghost sighting means, but he keeps silent. He knows that the ghosts were the men of the *Speedwell*, which now lay stricken, deep below the waves, on the ocean floor.

Unburied, the ghosts were restless. When the *Maria* passed above, the spectral sailors climbed aboard.

When the *Maria* returned to port, her entire crew deserted. They all believed that once a sailor sees a ghost, they too will soon be dead. As the story of the *Speedwell* ghosts spread in the port town, the captain could not find another crew. Even the most pitiful wretches along the docks would not sign up to work on the *Maria*. Eventually, the *Maria* was abandoned and she rotted away at her mooring and sank to the murky depths.

The ship Maria, was boarded by the ghost crew
of the sunken ship Speedwell.

THE MYSTERIOUS SEA

Since humanity first went down to the sea in ships, tales of sea ghosts have been told by sailors everywhere. In past centuries, the mysteries of the sea were beyond human control or understanding. As ships skimmed the vast surface of an ever-changing, unknown ocean, sailors never knew what fates awaited them. One day the breezes blow sweet and fair, guiding the ship through the magic, blue sea. Then, for reasons no one can fathom, the winds might stop, leaving the ship helplessly stranded beneath the withering sun. Starvation and disease soon tested the strength and loyalty of the crew. Worst of all, a gale could blow out of nowhere, tossing the ship about like a toy in the hands of an angry child.

Death was always lurking beneath the crystalline waves of the ocean. Even today, in the waters of the North, dense fog and mammoth icebergs reduce ships to splintered wreckage. North of Norway, vicious currents cause deadly whirlpools called maelstroms. Around the southern tip of Africa, westerly winds cause seventy-foot waves that can destroy any ship.

The sea can turn wicked in a matter of minutes.

WATERY DEATHS

To sailors of old, drowning seemed the most horrible death. So great was the fear of the ocean, that many sailors never learned to swim.

Sailors of old feared the sea so much that they rarely learned to swim. They would rather die quickly than float for hours on the relentless sea.

They thought it was better to drown quickly than to float for hours, fighting the relentless power of the sea. People were also afraid to rescue those drowning. It was believed that if the sea was cheated of one life, it would soon seek another.

And oh, the misery of death by water. The ice-cold fingers of the sea drag men down to the unloving heart of the ocean's floor. Drowning lungs fill with salty water. Far from the sun, a sailor's body sinks into a watery grave. Rooted to the ocean floor, dead sailors rock in the current, never sleeping, never free, their souls restlessly haunting the surface, begging for release.

Seafarers call this grave Davy Jones's locker. Some believe that the word "Davy" comes from "duffy," a word in African slave dialect that means "ghost." "Jones" comes from the biblical Jonah, who was sacrificed to the sea by sailors trying to escape a storm. Jonah was swallowed by a whale, so Jonah's "locker" is the belly of the beast. Others believe that the term comes from the Hindu goddess of death, Deva Lokka. Whatever the origins of the term, the thought of Davy Jones's locker strikes terror into even the most seasoned sailor.

BLESS THIS SHIP

Those who lived their lives on the sea —
merchants, sailors, fishermen, and explorers —
used many rituals to protect themselves. In many
countries, ships were built on sacred ground that
was dedicated to the gods. In northern European
countries, shipbuilding was started on
Wednesday, because it was the day named for
Woden, the supreme god. Shipbuilding was never
started on Thursday, named for Thor, the god of
storms. Nor was it started on Friday, the day
named for the Goddess Freyda, who collected
human souls.

Many believed that ships were blessed or cursed
depending on the wood used in their
construction. Oak was used in shipbuilding
because it was worshipped by the Vikings, Gauls,
Greeks, and Romans. Oak was also thought to
protect ships against lightning. Holly was thought
to protect ships against evil. Black walnut was
never used because it was said to be the Devil's
tree and a lightning attractor. Once a ship was
finished, *eyes* were painted on its bow to ward off
evil. In later times, a carved wooden bust of a

woman was placed on the bow to offer protection.

More ceremonies began when a ship was ready to be launched. Shipwrights prayed that flocks of seagulls would circle overhead, for they were thought to be the friendly souls of dead sailors, and their cries were a blessing. Vikings splattered their ships with the blood of human sacrifices. Greeks used animal blood. In later times, wine was used to simulate blood. Today, a ship is christened with champagne, following a tradition that dates back thousands of years.

After the ship was launched, more superstitions were used for protection. Golden earrings in sailors' ears helped keep a ship afloat. Iron horseshoes under a deck brought good luck. Brooms were nailed to masts to sweep in good winds. Sailors never whistled on board because that was thought to call up a strong wind. Above all, no dead man could be kept on a ship. Captains knew that the presence of a coffin on board would cause a mutiny. When the dead were near, the sea would attack, so sailors gave corpses directly to the sea.

13

When someone died on a ship, they were washed and dressed, and sewn in a shroud. Shackles were chained to their feet so that they would sink into the depths and never be able to rise from the sea to haunt the living. The corpse was slipped into the water while the sailors mourned. But if the dead man had been murdered or had died in battle, its ghost might drift about for centuries, tormenting all who saw it. The sight of pale faces and dripping bodies rising from the sea chilled all, because they knew that the sea was ever-hungry for fresh bodies. Disaster was sure to follow.

THE *FLYING DUTCHMAN*

One of the most famous ghost ships sailing the high seas is the *Flying Dutchman*. The specter of this ship haunts the Cape of Good Hope, at the southern tip of Africa. The first time the *Flying Dutchman* was sighted was in the late 1600s. The men that spotted her said that although the weather was good and the sea calm, the *Flying Dutchman* appeared to be battling her way through a violent gale.

Legend has it that the *Flying Dutchman* was making its voyage around the cape when it ran into a wind "strong enough to blow the horns off a bull." Although the ship was in danger, her captain, Captain Vanderdecken refused to turn back or seek port. When the passengers pleaded with Captain Vanderdecken to save them, he laughed in their faces and sang songs of a "horrible and blasphemous nature." The ship was buffeted by the wind and her masts were blown clear off. Vanderdecken sat in his cabin, puffing a pipe and drinking rum. When the passengers tried to force the captain to go back, he threw their leader overboard.

One of the most famous ghost ships is
the Flying Dutchman

Even as the screams of the drowning man filled the air, the clouds opened up and a form alighted on the deck. The form is said to have been the "Almighty Himself." The passengers trembled with fear, but the captain continued to puff his pipe defiantly. The form said, "Captain, you are very stubborn."

"And you are a rascal," the captain replied. "Who wants a peaceful passage? I don't. I'm asking nothing of you, so clear out or I'll blow your brains out."

The captain drew his pistol and fired at the form, but the pistol exploded in his hand. The form told him that henceforth he was accursed, condemned to sail forever without rest.

"Bitterness shall be your drink," said the form, "and red hot iron shall be your meat. Only your cabin boy shall remain with you, and horns will grow out of the middle of his head. He shall have a muzzle like a tiger and skin rougher than a dogfish. And since it is your delight to torment sailors, torment them you shall. For you will be the evil spirit of the sea and your ship will bring misfortune to all who sight it."

Thus the story of the *Flying Dutchman* began. The *Flying Dutchman* was blamed for casting many ships into uncharted waters and breaking them upon the rocks. On any of the Seven Seas, Captain Vanderdecken made trouble by turning wine into vinegar and curdling a ship's food into rotting beans. Sometimes a phantom boat would cast off from the *Flying Dutchman* and innocently approach a ship. This was a sure sign of doom. Some sailors thought that the evil captain had repented. Sometimes sailors saw him standing on the *Flying Dutchman* with his head lying beside him on the deck. The head would plead to God for mercy while a crew of skeleton sailors laughed.

The curse of the *Flying Dutchman* spread like a disease to all who encountered her. On May 4, 1866, the sailing ship *General Grant,* out of Melbourne, Australia and bound for London, was making good headway. For no reason, on May 13 she found herself stranded on the equator with no wind. This was a mystery, because this area was known for good trade winds. Somehow, the *General Grant* was pushed along by some unknown force. Soon, she piled into the cliffs of Disappointment Island, so named because of all the disasters that happened and ghosts lurking there. For several previous days, the *General Grant* had been followed by a mystery ship that many believed was the *Flying Dutchman.* In the cabin safe of the *General Grant* was one million dollars in gold. For the next one hundred years, everyone who tried to recover that gold met with disaster and death.

Newspapers reported *Flying Dutchman* sightings in 1893, 1905, and 1911. During the 1940s, several commanders of German submarines spotted the *Flying Dutchman* as they fought in World War II sea battles. No one knows the exact number of those submarine sailors who perished in the watery depths.

THE CASE OF THE HEADLESS SAILOR

In the early 1890s, the docks of San Francisco, California, were awash with busted gold panners, wealthy merchants, roustabout cowboys, and at least one headless sailor. This very strange affair all started aboard the Norwegian freighter *Squanto,* in 1892.

One night, when the *Squanto* was docked in San Francisco's harbor, the first mate, Andrew Wilder, was murdered. His body was found floating headless in the water. It seems that the sailor had been done in by the *Squanto's* captain, Jack Rand, who disliked the sailor intensely, and Rand's wife, Betsy. On that fateful evening, Captain Rand plied the first mate with drink. When Wilder passed out, Betsy held the poor sailor's arms while Captain Rand chopped off Wilder's head with an axe. Many believe that Betsy Rand and Wilder were in love. Fearing that her affair might be found out, Betsy Rand helped the captain kill her lover.

Soon after the gruesome murder, the *Squanto* set sail for the long, treacherous journey to New Brunswick, Canada. The trip could take as long as twelve months, because the ship had to sail all the way down the west coast of South America, around the dangerous Cape Horn at the southern tip of the continent, and then 12,000 miles north to Canada. The crew was stuck on board, with not much to do and a lot of time to think. And they were carrying more than cargo. They were also carrying the headless ghost of Andrew Wilder.

Somewhere at the beginning of the *Squanto's* journey, Captain Rand was killed in a mutiny. The captain who replaced him was also killed. The reasons for the killing of the two captains were never quite clear, but many believe it had to do with the odd happenings relating to Wilder's ghost. In this bizarre manner, two more captains wound up dead. When the *Squanto* reached New Brunswick in early 1893, the entire crew deserted her. Efforts to find another crew proved futile, and the ship sat idle for a long time.

Captain Rand, of the ship Squanto, murdered his
first mate, Andrew Wilder; this caused a series of
chilling ghost sightings.

Eventually, rumors of the ship's haunting reached the Norwegian Consul, who decided to investigate. Two hard-headed, burly seamen were hired as night watchmen for the *Squanto*. They were instructed to hide aboard the ship and watch for anything unusual. Anyone caught playing tricks on the ship was to be arrested.

The two men rowed out to the *Squanto* about 9 p.m. and hid in the cabin. For an hour, all was calm. Just as the two men started to believe that the hauntings were a hoax, they heard a series of odd noises on the deck. They ran to the deck and found chaos. When they had boarded, everything on the ship had been spic and span — neat, orderly and in place. Now, they found spars, ropes, yards, hand spikes, and barrels littered all over the deck. Not a soul was in sight. The guards were bewildered but tired, so they decided to turn in for the night.

The men had not been asleep for long when they were awakened by someone tugging at their sleeves. When they sat up, no one was there! When the men climbed out of their bunks, cold, unseen hands brushed their faces. A chilling, hollow whisper rang through the cabin, "Go, go at once!" The men did not need to be told twice, they ran from the cabin and started for their skiff.

They heard a crash behind them. When they turned around in the pale, misty light, they saw a headless figure lumbering toward them carrying its head under its arm. It was the ghost of Andrew Wilder. As the guards stood frozen in terror, Wilder grabbed his head in his hands and heaved it at the screaming men. The bloody head, stopped directly in front of their faces while its gaping mouth let out a blood-curdling scream. Then, it passed right through the men, crashed onto the deck, and disappeared. The watchmen jumped overboard and swam towards shore. But the water was cold, and waves dragged them down. The bodies of the two men were found washed ashore the next morning with expressions of fear still frozen on their bloated faces.

No one ever returned to the *Squanto,* and it finally sank into the cold Atlantic Ocean, with its headless sailor still on board. That seemed to be the end of Andrew Wilder, but no one knows for sure.

The ghost of Andrew Wilder, holding his head under his arm.

ＫSHIRE JACK AND SARAH

ι ever walked along the seashore at dusk ᴜ...ᴇ... d eerie noises blowing over the waves? Was it a seagull crying or was it the sound of the wind and the waves? Or was it the cry of a man who drowned long ago when his ship went down? Could it be the screams of a drowning woman who threw herself into the waves when her man did not return from the sea? It's all part of the mystery of the sea.

One voice that many fishermen in northeastern England still hear calling from the sea is that of Yorkshire Jack. Yorkshire, England, is probably one of the most haunted areas of the world, and Jack is just one of the area's famous ghosts.

The story of Yorkshire Jack begins with a lovely young woman named Sarah Polgrain who lived in the town of Ludgvan in the early 1800s. Sarah was married to George Polgrain, who was nearly forty years older than his wife. Having long lost whatever love she had for her husband, Sarah took up with Yorkshire Jack, who was more her own age. After she began to see Jack, Sarah quarreled every day with her husband. Neighbors got used to the sound of breaking dishes and screams coming from the Polgrain's home.

On one morning, however, Sarah rushed to her neighbor's cottage pale and shaken. She said George had been taken ill. Later, Sarah's neighbor learned that George had died. At that time, no one suspected foul play. The doctor signed the death certificate, and George was buried. Shortly after the funeral though, rumors of murder began to circulate.

Local authorities heard the rumors and decided to dig up George's corpse and give it a thorough medical examination. His body was found to contain enough arsenic to kill six men. Sarah was arrested, charged with murder, tried, and found guilty. As punishment, she was sentenced to hang from the neck until dead.

On the day of her hanging, Sarah had one last request. She asked if Yorkshire Jack could accompany her to the gallows. The request was granted and Jack was permitted to mount the platform of the scaffold. As the rope was placed around Sarah's neck, Jack kissed her and the two embraced for the last time. Sarah whispered a question to Jack, to which he replied nervously, "I will."

After the execution, Sarah's ghost was seen around town. It was spotted once in the churchyard by the cemetery and once on a road near town. When Yorkshire Jack heard of the sightings, he seemed very disturbed. Jack's friends noticed a change in the young sailor. He was no longer cheerful and the life of the party. He became quite sour-tempered and bleak. His fresh-looking complexion turned to a ghostly pallor. Wherever Jack went, he constantly looked over his shoulder. One night at the local pub, Jack admitted to some friends: "She gives me no peace. Wherever I go she follows me. Wherever I turn, I find her at my elbow." Everyone knew that "she" was Sarah Polgrain.

Jack went back to sea, but the strange presence followed him. His shipmates also became aware of the presence in their midst. This went on for months until the ship returned to port. On that day, Jack confessed to his shipmates that when he stood on the gallows with Sarah, she had made him promise he would marry her.

Yorkshire Jack was forever burdened
by the ghost of Sarah Polgrain

He thought that Sarah's mind was unhinged and, trying to humor her, he had agreed. But Jack decided that Sarah was quite sane. Not being able to wed him in the flesh, Sarah meant to bind him to her forever in spirit. And that night at midnight was to be their wedding!

Jack's shipmates were awakened by the sound of high-heeled shoes. At 12 o'clock that night, the tap, tap, tapping stopped beside Yorkshire Jack's hammock. Trembling, his face distorted with fear, Jack arose and went onto the deck. The tapping followed him. Once on deck, Jack climbed up the mast and dove into the sea. His shipmates briefly saw two white faces bobbing among the black billows of the waves. Then they were gone.

Far away, Jack's friends could hear the chiming of church bells. All believed that they were Jack and Sarah's wedding bells. To this very day, fishermen hear the chiming of the bells in the sea, and the cries of Jack's forlorn voice shouting, "I do, I do!"

Yorkshire Jack dove into the sea after the ghost of Sarah Polgrain.

GONE WITH THE TIDES

Stories of ghost ships and ghost sailors are as old as the sea itself. While boats have become safer in modern times, hundreds of people are still lost at sea each year. That is why the Seven Seas will remain haunted for all of eternity. From the Pacific to the Atlantic to the Indian Ocean to the China Sea, phantoms of the deep will still demand another sailor, another ship. So when you're walking on the beach or sailing on the sea, keep your eyes and ears open. That boat on the horizon may be the *Flying Dutchman.* Just say, "Ship ahoy, matey." And tell 'em Yorkshire Jack sent you!